GAMBLED ON MY SORROW & CAME OUT WITH GRACE

Josefina Santiago

BookLeaf Publishing

India | USA | UK

Gambled on my sorrow & came out with grace

© 2021 Josefina Santiago

All rights reserved.

No part of this publication may be reproduced, stored in a retrieval system, or transmitted, in any form or by any means, electronic, mechanical, photocopying, recording or otherwise, without the prior written permission of the presenters.

Josefina Santiago asserts the moral right to be identified as author of this work.

Presentation by *BookLeaf Publishing*

Web: www.bookleafpub.com

E-mail: info@bookleafpub.com

ISBN: 9789358360486

First edition 2021

1.

HERSELF-

One day she woke up, walked to the mirror, looked up & saw something...

She saw herself, she really sees herself, something about herself, she was amazed of what she discovered within herself...

Deeper she stares, perplexed by what she sees, wondering why she's been abandoned and seeks compassion...

Life has put her on a journey that she could not imagine...

She punishes herself, insults herself, tries not to be herself...

The dark circles under her eyes, the wrinkles on her forehead from constant thinking, stressing, regressing...

But still she continues to look at herself, As time rounds the clock & days become night she realizes that she's changed herself, she has found herself...

She likes what she sees, she has a story to tell, she finds her smile... impressive...

She talks to herself, interesting... winks at herself, faces herself, is no longer afraid of herself....

No more quick looks, no longer will I turn my back on myself, no I will not stop with just a glance....

She looks good at herself, puts lipstick on, blushes her cheeks....I don't need no one else she's says to herself, she can do it, without giving it a second thought, now life looks a little enhanced....

She finally finds herself....everyday is a journey she reminds herself, lessons learned, mistakes made & forgiveness for herself....

"Love" love for herself....it feels strange to know one self, to recognize yourself....to find yourself....to finally discover yourself "worth".

2.

HOLES-

When I walked in the room the energy was strong...

It was full of smoke...

Smell of cigars & cigarettes fill the air...

Drinks were flowing...

I was just glowing...

In my element...

My inspiration, my reason for existence...

I was brought here for a reason...

Until this moment I didn't realize what my purpose was until the first word...

The spoken word that echoed throughout the space that seemed to surround me...

It captivated me...

I felt as if I was the only soul in that room & it was meant for me...

I needed to step up...

I wanted to be on that center stage...

Releasing all of what I have to offer verbally...

I want all the snaps, claps, oohs & aahs...

I want to share my words...

No longer do I want to keep it trapped or all in wraps...

My words are wanting to get out...

Deep breath, sigh...

I grabbed the mic and my stomach churned...

Can't stop now it was my turn...

I let my voice carry out what I wanted to say...

This was my day...

And when it was all said & done I was no longer afraid...

No way, not today...

I had spoken...

Life would never be the same...

I said what I said...

I recited what I recited...

Word for word filled the air...

Did I dare to make my dreams come true...

And I did...

To be fair & truthful I got off that stage with no oohs, nor aahs not even a snap...

I didn't hang my head down... Because as I step down I straighten my crown & I hear a clap followed by another & another...

I came to listen but they came to hear...

To hear my spoken word...

Let the story be told...

My life changed forever in a little place called Holes.

3.

ONCE IN A LIFETIME-

Once in a lifetime take a chance...

Run through a meadow...

Play in the sand...

Make a snow angel...

Come on, take my hand...

So just jump out of a plane...

Look down at all the land...

Swim with the sharks...

Catch fireflies in the dark...

Dance in the rain...

Just once go ahead don't be afraid...

Take that chance to see what you made...

A lifetime of memories that will never fade...

Kiss a stranger...

Hug a bear...

Build a castle...

Ride a roller coaster no one will care...

Go play & create what's meant to be shared...

It's only once in a lifetime, let's be fair...

Zip lining in the biggest jungle...

Surfing the gnarly waves...

Just falling in love....

It's a chance to take just once, it's what we crave...

Holding your child for the first time...

Saving a life...

Putting out a fire...

An opportunity to just try & never get tired...

We all have it...

So don't let it pass you...

There might not be another chance
because it only comes...

Once in a lifetime.

4.

MY GRANDBABY-

Can't believe you are here...

I've been waiting for years... Your smile...

Your skin...

Your tiny toes & tiny feet...

Oh my this is such a treat...

I think we are going to be best friends and I will get you all the ice cream you can eat...

You can tell me anything...

Even if you think it's bad I will help you understand...

I will hug you...

I will kiss you...

And at times seem annoying but I want you to know I will always be here for you because my love for you will just keep growing...

How very blessed I am...

You are my little lamb...

My chunky monkey...

I feel so lucky...

We'll sit in the kitchen and I'll teach you how to bake...

Maybe some cakes or some chocolate shakes...

Whatever is your taste...

You have me wrapped around your finger...

I will lay you down & sing you a lullaby...

Read you a book... I will never leave your side...

Even when I leave this earth all you have to do is call on me...

I will not be far...

I never imagined I can love someone so much as I do you...

My forever little boo...

My grandbaby, this poem is for you.

5.

WRITERS BLOCK-

My head is on lock...

I can't focus. I feel as if I got hit with a rock...

I can hear the clock...it goes tick tock...

This mental block has stopped me...

Ahhh I know what I can do, maybe listen to a little hip hop...

Some jazz...

I'll try not to spazz...

I need to relax...

Jump around to some pop to get my mind going...

Then all the words will start flowing...

My creativity is growing...

I feel my inner book flipping pages...

I go into rages because I can't seem to get myself out of these blank stages...

I know I can release myself from these block cages...

Concentration is my key...

I have the power to unlock this you see...

Only I can release me...

Show you what I have inside and what I can be...

As I try to figure this out...

I need for you to understand what I'm all about...

I'm a peacemaker...

I'm a sister...

A mother...

A fighter... A lover...

But most of all I'm a writer...

As I fight this block I see the light...

I finally realize I don't need to fight...

I cleared my mind...

I started to write...

All this time I had it in me...

I just need to unlock this Writer's block.

6.

BELIEVE-

Believe in something higher...

Dream something amazing...

Become something new...

Reinvent yourself into something cool...

The universe is always talking to you...

Reaching out for you to be something grand...

Come on, I'll hold your hand...

Do something that changes lives...

Be that something you wish you always were...

I can see it in your eyes...

There's something about you that's terrific...

You can be something fantastic...

Just do something drastic...

Trust yourself...

Listen to your gut...

Even if you feel like you get into a rut...

Pull yourself out and up...

Because I believe in you and you have the stuff...

Believe in you...

Believe in whatever you do...

Believe in that something and you will achieve it...

Reach your hand out and receive it...

All you have to do is believe in it.

7.

ARUBA-

Blue crystal waters...

As clear as the eye can see...

Sand white and pure...

Fresh enough to rub all over your body...

Free spa treatment as only nature can give...

Under this raging sun is where I want to live...

I want to stay here forever...

I Drowned myself in this weather...

People are so kind and sweet...

They bring you your drinks and all you can eat...

The national bird Shoko just dropped a feather...

I guess it's my lucky day. I'll wear in my straw hat that's just like a sombrero...

Cocktails are flowing and music is playing...

Dancing is a must...

You just can't help yourself but to move your hips and give a little pelvic thrust...

Food tastes as good as it smells...

Seafood galore...

Oh no what's that I hear the bells and the horn...

It's time for me to go but I will walk slowly...

Hopefully it won't come to an end but wishful thinking is not my friend...

Reality hits hard and I know I must go now but before I do I'm going to send myself a card...

So I will always remember this place and the smile you put on my face...

The horn blows some more sounds just like a tuba...

I have reached my ship just in time but sadness falls upon me...

I'll miss you but I shall return...

Till next time, Aruba.

8.

LESSONS LEARNED-

I let you stay not because I'm weak...

I gave you time not because I was meek...

Ahhh little boy look at me as I tap you on your cheek...

You took my kindness...

But I shall not show you my weakness...

Because you see I am confident in being me...

I am beyond proud of what I achieve...

The blessings shall always be received...

You can not deter me from my beliefs...

The continuation of my giving is what I release...

From within me I am a good person...

Your bad luck will just worsen...

Lessons learned is what I'm going to teach you...

You can't just go around hurting or taking from people...

One thing you can expect is karma and she will reach you...

Can you really be a man if your mother is still holding your hand...

Your time is up, no more taking advantage...

You have always been just average...

No more chances given and when you finally realize what you have done...

It's better that you run and hide...

You are just a lie...

This is my time...

I am cleansed and brand new...

I have taken out the trash...

Just like a flash I am back to being glad...

You keep running your scams because I'm happy with who I am...

Generous, beautiful, strong, smart and most of all fearless...

Never be afraid to be you...

Continue to give and let live...

Lessons learned.

9.

ENDLESS-

Make it continuous, everlasting & contagious...

It should last forever and never stop...

Let light shine and pop...

Bright as the stars...

Shine like the moon...

You should feel it in your favorite tune...

luminescence is so bright that it exhibits the very essence of how you feel...

Make that deal...

Take a chance...

Take that ride on romance...

You feel it deep within and it's hot...

For what's burning within you is kismet...

You will feel that alot...

For when you both came together it was cataclysmic...

Fireworks exploding and shooting stars falling...

This is how it is when calling out to the world...

Let them know how you feel and how your love just twirls...

It's deep so let it be known...

This love will never finish...

It's more than you will ever know...

It is forever and forever more...

I promise to never be reckless or careless with you because this love we share is Endless.

10.

BROKEN PRINCESS-

I tend to wonder what happened to my crown as I look around the damp dark room.

They told me that I was lucky.

All I can see is sadness and gloom.

Little did they know that my life wasn't as simple as it seemed.

Smiles are not as big as you dreamed and the hugs are far and in between.

I look down and wonder if I would ever be seen.

Will my prince ever come and take me away from this evil queen?

I guess for now I shall wait. I will always ponder about my fate.

As I look around I dust off my crown, I step out of the room, I look around and I do the only thing I was taught to do...

Fake it so the people can continue to believe how lucky we are... That's how my life has been thus far.

11.

THE MESS-

Must begin to clean but I am getting mean looking at this mess...

Oh yes he has left me with his mess... So have the children those little pests leaving me also with their mess...

I can't seem to get my rest...

But why stress when I know that it will always be there, my mess...

Oh yes the one thing I can count on when the husband and children have left is my mess...

It will not complain nor be a pain in the neck and peck at my soul because I can have control...

Control over this mess...

Once they leave and I begin to clean my head will hurt less...

But you know it can wait then I can take...

Take my time because it will be fine after all it is all mine my mess I guess...

I'll take a little rest because it will always be there, my mess...

One thing I know it will never fail me and it will always be there...

I guess it's time...

Time to clean up this mess...

It has been 10 minutes later and some progress...

My little family will be home soon...

Let's see how long this will last...

They don't seem impressed because of course they love the mess...

Nonetheless it's ok I guess because after all it is all my mess.

12.

SWEET SIXTEEN-

Sweet sixteen you are now more than a little girl...

You are now a young woman...

With hopes and dreams...

Imagination supreme...

My sweet sixteen you can be whatever you choose to be...

The world is opening up new things you will see...

Your beauty shows and you radiate all over the place...

Wherever you go they see your shine...

Take your time sweet sixteen this is not a race...

Everyone can tell when you leave a trace...

Because your smells are like honeysuckle in spring...

Your eyes are glossy like the dew after a morning rain shower...

My sweet sixteen I think you have a thing...

If I could I would build a tower...

To hide you away so no one can hurt you but what good would that be...

After all, I want to share you, my growing flower...

I know you have the power...

To guard yourself and be aware of things that are sour...

I don't want to let go...

It's time though...

Let me put your crown on and your glass slippers...

Gather around now in a row...

Here comes my princess with all her glow...

Happy birthday sweet sixteen, enjoy because this is your show.

13.

LOCK DOWN-

Lock down, lock down and run into your house.

Lock your doors.

Close your windows.

My brothers and sisters are being shot.

The virus is coming in hot, shelter in place and cover your face.

You could get killed right in your own place.

Shit is real.

Are you ready to deal?

Is this going to be our last meal?

Oh Lord Father come save us my people are dying I'm not lying...

Lock down, lock down got me so depressed.

Nowhere to go.

Nowhere to turn.

Look into your mirror and stare at yourself.

Who were you before all this. Being shut out and closed in.

It will make you stressed. Sad to see so much death.

Mad for innocent killing.

Our hearts keep reeling and the tears keep falling...

Lock down, lock down this is all just hate.

We need to stop stalling.

Love our planet and be kind to one another.

Treasure our blessings this is our calling.

Repent our actions and change our ways.

Love one another and help each other.

If you can't see what I see then there's no hope.

We won't survive, we are doomed...

Lock down lock down we can't sit and just mope.

There has to be hope.

We have to break down the walls.

Open the windows and step outside.

Take that deep breath and make change for our people.

For our health and for our planet or else we are all going to regret it...

Lock down, lock down what you have taught us is grace.

To be humble.

To love one another because tomorrow is not promised.

Forever can quickly turn into never.

So let's not forget it.

Wear your mask, wash your hands and be kind to your fellow man.

Feed our animals and help mother earth because we can't continue to be shut down.

Let's release our minds so we can end this Lockdown.

14.

DREAMY STATE-

Hanging by a string my heart starts to beat...

Rain drops begin to fall...

I can feel the warm heat with my face in the air...

I can hear the birds peep...

Listen to them chirp...

Oh how I love you mother earth...

 I wonder what they seek...

They may want to soar high into the sky..

Beyond these streets...

The sounds are enlightening me...

Life changing...

Rotating cycle that takes different forms...

I'm enjoying the effervescence of life perform...

What we have been blessed with is so amazing...

I can see the cows grazing...

In the distance not far behind is a willow tree...

I take this sight with ease...

Enjoying this breeze...

This jaunt I have taken has pleased me...

I enjoy what I see and feel so free.

Appreciate and alleviate...

Get out and enjoy your dreamy state.

15

BRICK CITY-

Brick city is where I come from...

Down the block from the corner bodega...

Gotta use the pay phone because money is tight and we can't afford one at home...

This is the city where I roam...

Waiting on the lines takes so long but mommy says we need cheese and milk it's free from the government you see...

Another brother shot...

Another mother left alone pregnant and ready to pop...

Hit the candy shop for a five cent lollipop...

That's all I got...

It's rough in these streets but this is where I love to be...

Sirens at night and sirens at day...

I ain't going to stay...

Not forever anyways...

Gotta finish school and then get out of here...

Ah shit gotta go get my brother's beer...

Step over the body...

Who knows if he's dead...

I feel like he's been here for years...

Cops don't care, they want us to live in fear...

Smoke that dope and drink that lean...

That's who we are or that's what they think...

I mean...

No one cares for the city, it's survival of the fittest...

These streets took my brother and my homie too...

damn dude...

Sorry if you think I'm rude but this is the only way to be in this hood...

You are not welcome here...

Walk away before they shed blood...

Cold as ice and hot as hell...

The dap of the hand is the way they can tell...

 If you belong here or you are trying to cause some problems there...

Wait what's that smell...

Jamaican food...

Spanish food...

Some pizza or some egg rolls...

 Just changed my mood...

So good...

I'll play some skelly later...

Maybe some double dutch...

I'm not in a rush... Just a kid trying to live...

My neighbors know me...

Their neighbors know them...

Mess around and get in trouble...

Your momma will know because the neighbors will tell them so...

Johnny pumps open, gonna get my feet wet...

Sit on the stoop and watch the people go step by step...

 Ice cream they shout...

The one thing we can count on is for that truck to be on time...

If only it was safe...

I would stay...

Everything is made of concrete with the exception of that one tree on the corner that sways...

Pop some change in my man's cup...

Time to head in...

Can't be caught outside when that street light comes on...

It's different at night...

My mom wants me to be alright...

So I head in...

Eat some rice and beans...

Shower and brush my teeth...

Lay down and say my prayers...

Cover myself with this one layer...

Look out the window...

See the moon shining...

It looks so pretty...

I say to myself no matter where I go or where life might take me I will always be part of this beautiful brick city.

16.

THAT MONKEY IS MY FRIEND-

He had come to play...

This little funny monkey...

Silly buddy of mine...

Every time he wants to tickle...

Jump & play... Run & hide... Don't get him wrong he can be a little fickle... He laughs...

He swings...

I hung up some rings so he could do his thing...

He cuddles...

He eats...

The bananas and oranges are his favorite...

I like to give him little treats...

My monkey is so sweet...

My best friend shows exuberance. I must nature it...

I'm so lucky to have you...

Come hold my hand with that strong grip...

We'll skip along and take a little trip...

Be with me forever...

Here, take a sip...

This drink is cold...

You will be mine to hold...

My funny monkey of mine...

This friendship will last us to the end of time.

17.

SAD LOVE STORY-

I wish it didn't have to be this way...

That we can love each other like we used to...

Bring back the time of laughter and joy...

of silliness...

of something so pure and true...

I miss you, my best friend...

I don't know why it had to end...

If your heart is broken I have one to lend...

Time stands still, it never bends...

That's how this love grew...

Into something that no one could understand or comprehend...

They can't see how intense our energy is for each other...

Even if there was a rumble or a stumble in our path we would still find our way back...

I dream that we will return... maybe not in the same way as before but into something much more...

For we can defeat these odds of anyone believing love is hard...

I couldn't understand why the universe put us on this journey but I'm all for our love taking another chance on our matrimony.

18.

FRUSTRATIONS-

When I start to feel like I hit a brick wall... I stop...

Take a deep breath and stand tall...

With all my might I make that shit fall...

Obstacles can be your worst enemy...

It's almost like you have to brawl just to crawl out of your own felony...

All I am seeking is my serenity...

My peace...

My somewhat of a happy place...

Or at least somewhere safe...

I have to seek my faith...

Just so I can escape...

Things don't seem to go my way but hey what can I say...

I create...

What I give out is what will come back to me...

So my abundance of giving and caring has to be genuine...

So that I can receive positivity...

At times it feels like you can't make it...

You just gotta shake it and break it...

Don't allow those voices to get in it...

Into your spirit...

Because it will consume you...

Change you into a monster...

All you are going to feel is used...

By the demons...

That leaves behind lesions...

I tell you to pray to your higher power so you can cleanse those adhesions...

Putting a bandaid on it doesn't make it go away...

It just deepens...

Trust me I'm talking to you as my friend...

If you don't listen you will be weakened...

It feels at times it's all coming to an end but you go on don't let that transcend...

Do you understand...

Life is a test and there's no time to waste...

If only we could forget like we forgive...

Then it would be easier to heal...

I'm gonna be real...

Try my hardest to not feel this struggle...

Even though in this bubble it is just me...

I can battle anything...

Just dont judge me...

We are alike you see...

So hold my hand...

Let's start walking...

We can get through anything as long as
we continue to stand together and keep
talking.

19.

DARKNESS-

All that darkness and not enough light...
All this anger and not enough peace...

Within is so much pain hidden away by
all that plight...

I often wonder if it's just better to give up
the fight...

There's so much gloom that it fills up the
room...

One day this will all come to an end
that's what they say anyways...

But at what cost and what day...

Tears fall...

We built a wall... Scared to continue at
all...

Day by day we wonder if we will
survive...

There's no more love, just greed and pestilence...

Whatever happened to our excellence...

The lowest form of existence...

All we can do is have faith and look to a higher power for guidance...

What we want is irrelevant and what we need is sufficient...

Let's be conformed to what is necessary to survive...

Our ancestors want us to derive what we learned into something that is continuously alive...

Maybe we'll find our way out and stop this decline...

The sun will shine and we'll be fine...

It's just wishful thinking...

We should be ambivalent to what we can change...

It can be strange but it is certainly something we can obtain...

I believe...

We all can achieve...

Out of darkness must come light...

So beyond these fights let's do what's right.

20.

LOVE ONE ANOTHER-

What do you care if I choose love and not hate...

Is it any of your business...

Should it even frustrate you what decisions I take...

You spend too much time wondering about my fate...

Live your life I say...

Mind your estate and keep your stones...

Throwing without knowing will only break your bones...

It hurts so bad...

What you can't control...

There's two people in love and not what is the norm...

She loves her and he loves him...

If they're in love with a tree or maybe someone who is chinese..

It's not your life so let them be...

If you want to disagree by all means...

Just have the respect to keep it to yourself and hide it inside deep...

Because love is love created for you and me...

So stop trying to change what you can't believe, let us just disagree...

You nor me can not decide if we're right or wrong only our savior can make those calls...

So when you think you need to say something rude let's just not say anything at all...

Let's just love each other...

Respect one another...

Let's not bother or create confusion...

At the end of the day they are all your mothers, sisters and brothers even if they are living under cover...

So they are not judged or prosecuted for loving him, her or however... Let love discover love...

Oh how wonderful this world would be if we would just accept what we really are and that's human beings...

We have the right to love who we are seeing...

Stop the misleading and start treating everyone with peace...

Once that all happens we will have love for all and that my friends are the most freeing...

21.

What do you care if I choose love and not hate...

Is it any of your business...

Should it even frustrate you what decisions I make...

You spend too much time wondering about my fate...

Live your life I say...

Mind your estate and keep your stones...

Throwing without knowing will only break your bones...

It hurts so bad...

What you can't control...

There's two people in love and not what is the norm...

She loves her and he loves him...

If they're in love with a tree or maybe someone who is chinese...

It's not your life so let them be...

If you want to disagree by all means...

Just have the respect to keep it to yourself and hide it inside deep...

Because love is love created for you and me...

So stop trying to change what you can't believe, let us just disagree...

You nor me can not decide if we're right or wrong only our savior can make those calls...

So when you think you need to say something rude let's just not say anything at all...

Let's just love each other...

Respect one another...

Let's not bother or create confusion...

At the end of the day they are all your mothers, sisters and brothers even if they are living under cover...

So let's not judge or prosecute for loving him, her or whomever... Let love discover love...

Oh how wonderful this world would be if we would just accept what we really are and that's human beings...

We have the right to love who we are seeing...

Stop the misleading and start treating everyone with peace...

Once that all happens we will have love for all and that my friends will be the most freeing.